Here Is the Coral Reef

Madeleine Dunphy

ILLUSTRATED BY Tom Leonard

Hyperion Books for Children
New York

Text © 1998 by Madeleine Dunphy.
Illustrations © 1998 by Tom Leonard.

Printed in Singapore.

FIRST EDITION
3 5 7 9 10 8 6 4

This book set in 14-Point Benguait.
Artwork is prepared using acrylic.

Library of Congress Cataloging-in-Publication Data

Dunphy, Madeleine.
Here is the coral reef / Madeleine Dunphy ; illustrated by Tom Leonard.
p.   cm.
Summary: Uses repeating text in a cumulative nursery rhyme to describe the relationships between
plants and animals in the ecology of a coral reef.
ISBN 0-7868-0163-8 (trade)--ISBN 0-7868-2135-3 (lib. bdg.)
1. Coral reef ecology--Australia--Great Barrier Reef (Qld.)--Juvenile literature. (I. Coral reef ecology.
2. Ecology.)
I. Leonard, Thomas, 1955-   . II. Title.
QH197.D85   1998
577.7'89'09943--dc21   97-20886

For Chris with love

—M. D.

For my parents,
Richard and Theresa

—T. L.

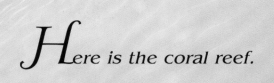

Here is the coral reef.

*H*ere is the coral
of all colors and shapes
that lives in clear waters
in this vivid seascape:
Here is the coral reef.

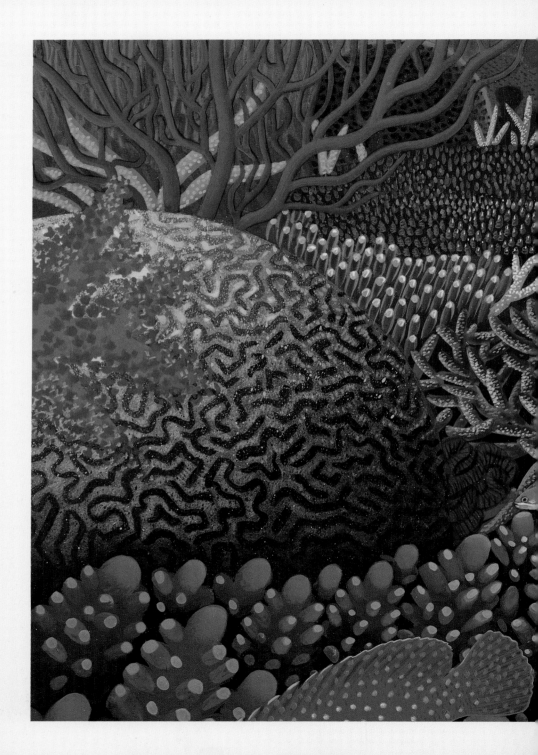

*H*ere are the parrotfish
who eat the coral
of all colors and shapes
that lives in clear waters
in this vivid seascape:
Here is the coral reef.

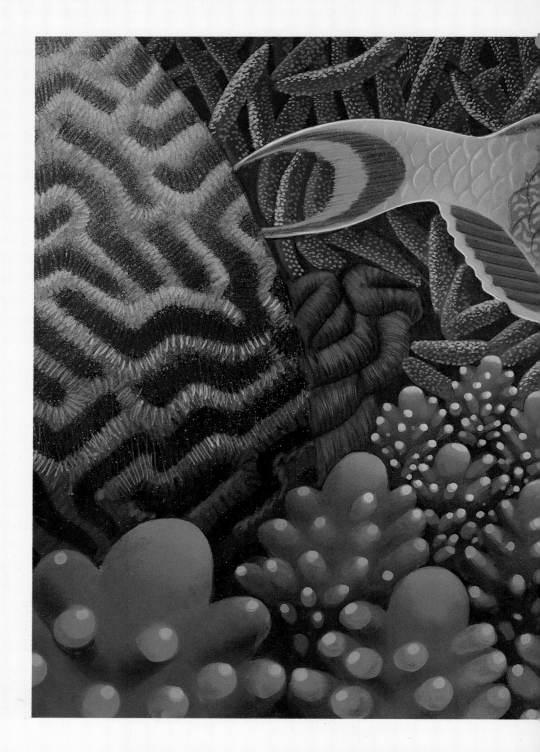

*H*ere are the wrasses
that clean the parrotfish
who eat the coral
of all colors and shapes
that lives in clear waters
in this vivid seascape:
Here is the coral reef.

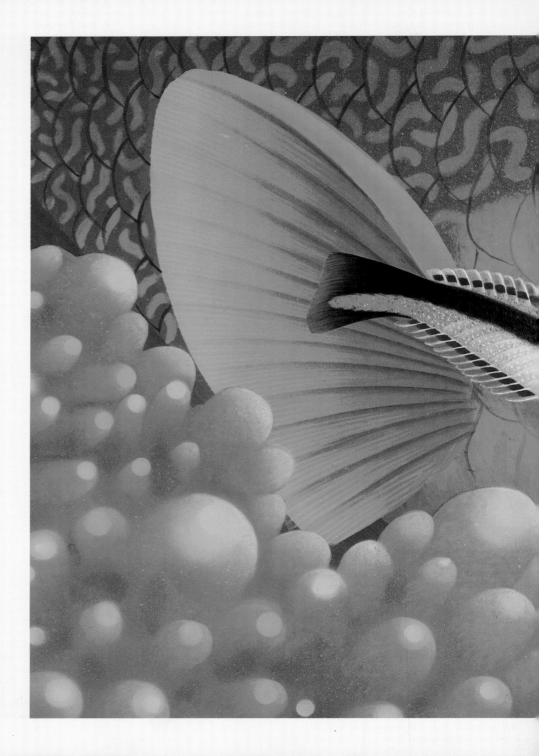

*H*ere is the cod

who is groomed by the wrasses

that clean the parrotfish

who eat the coral

of all colors and shapes

that lives in clear waters

in this vivid seascape:

Here is the coral reef.

Here is the anemone
that stings the cod

who is groomed by the wrasses

that clean the parrotfish

who eat the coral

of all colors and shapes

that lives in clear waters

in this vivid seascape:

Here is the coral reef.

Here are the clownfish

who hide in the anemone

that stings the cod

who is groomed by the wrasses

that clean the parrotfish

who eat the coral

of all colors and shapes

that lives in clear waters

in this vivid seascape:

Here is the coral reef.

*H*ere is the sponge

that lives near the clownfish

who hide in the anemone

that stings the cod

who is groomed by the wrasses

that clean the parrotfish

who eat the coral

of all colors and shapes

that lives in clear waters

in this vivid seascape:

Here is the coral reef.

_H_ere is the turtle

that nibbles the sponge

that lives near the clownfish

who hide in the anemone

that stings the cod

who is groomed by the wrasses

that clean the parrotfish

who eat the coral

of all colors and shapes

that lives in clear waters

in this vivid seascape:

Here is the coral reef.

*H*ere is the ray

who swims with the turtle

that nibbles the sponge

that lives near the clownfish

who hide in the anemone

that stings the cod

who is groomed by the wrasses

that clean the parrotfish

who eat the coral

of all colors and shapes

that lives in clear waters

in this vivid seascape:

Here is the coral reef.

Here are the remoras

that ride the ray

who swims with the turtle

that nibbles the sponge

that lives near the clownfish

who hide in the anemone

that stings the cod

who is groomed by the wrasses

that clean the parrotfish

who eat the coral

of all colors and shapes

that lives in clear waters

in this vivid seascape:

Here is the coral reef.

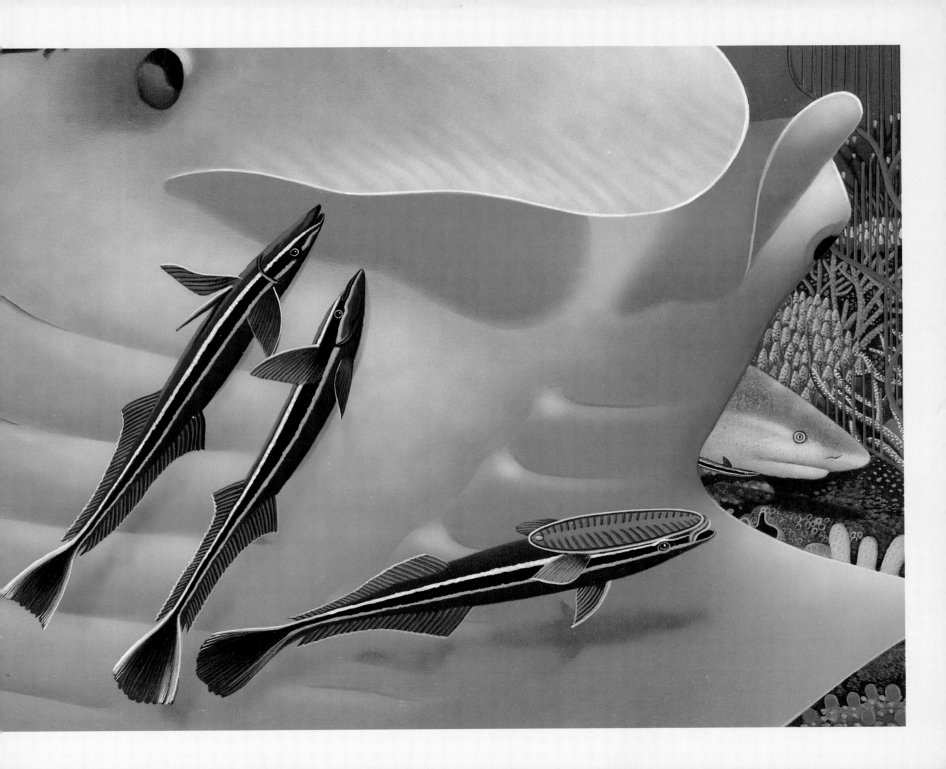

*H*ere is the shark
that carries the remoras
that ride the ray
who swims with the turtle
that nibbles the sponge
that lives near the clownfish
who hide in the anemone
that stings the cod
who is groomed by the wrasses
that clean the parrotfish
who eat the coral
of all colors and shapes
that lives in clear waters
in this vivid seascape:
Here is the coral reef.

*H*ere is the eel

who is attacked by the shark

that carries the remoras

that ride the ray

who swims with the turtle

that nibbles the sponge

that lives near the clownfish

who hide in the anemone

that stings the cod

who is groomed by the wrasses

that clean the parrotfish

who eat the coral

of all colors and shapes

that lives in clear waters

in this vivid seascape:

Here is the coral reef.

Here is the coral
that shelters the eel
who is attacked by the shark
that carries the remoras
that ride the ray
who swims with the turtle
that nibbles the sponge
that lives near the clownfish
who hide in the anemone
that stings the cod
who is groomed by the wrasses
that clean the parrotfish
who eat the coral
of all colors and shapes
that lives in clear waters
in this vivid seascape:
Here is the coral reef.

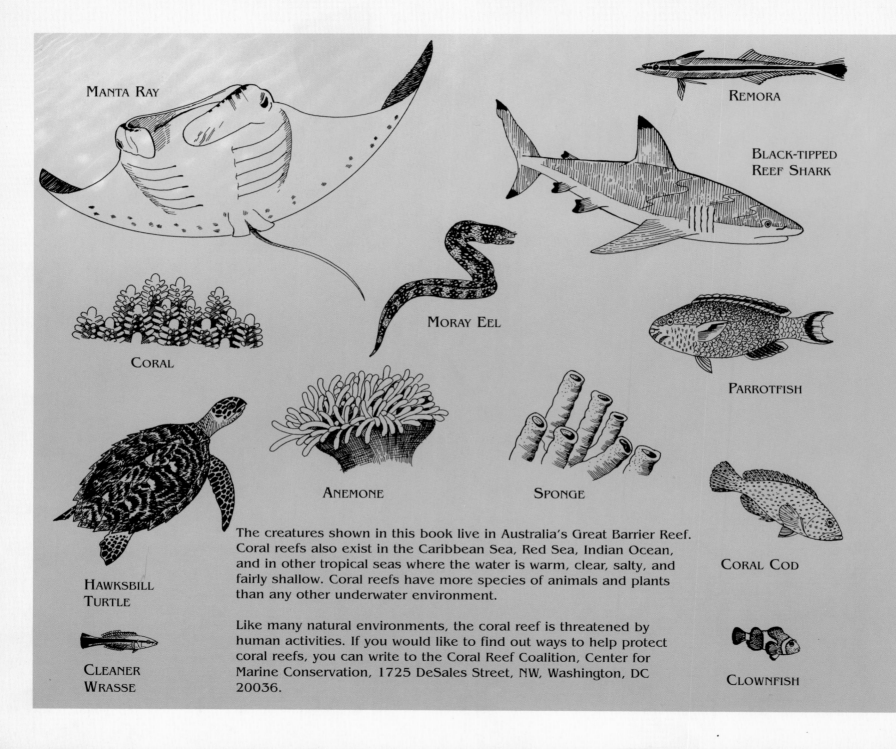

MANTA RAY

REMORA

BLACK-TIPPED REEF SHARK

MORAY EEL

CORAL

PARROTFISH

ANEMONE

SPONGE

HAWKSBILL TURTLE

CORAL COD

The creatures shown in this book live in Australia's Great Barrier Reef. Coral reefs also exist in the Caribbean Sea, Red Sea, Indian Ocean, and in other tropical seas where the water is warm, clear, salty, and fairly shallow. Coral reefs have more species of animals and plants than any other underwater environment.

Like many natural environments, the coral reef is threatened by human activities. If you would like to find out ways to help protect coral reefs, you can write to the Coral Reef Coalition, Center for Marine Conservation, 1725 DeSales Street, NW, Washington, DC 20036.

CLEANER WRASSE

CLOWNFISH